Emily Is Being Bullied,
What Can She Do?

Emily Is Being Bullied, What Can She Do?

A Story and Anti-Bullying Guide for Children and Adults to Read Together

HELEN COWIE, HARRIET TENENBAUM
AND FFION JONES

Illustrated by Ffion Jones

Jessica Kingsley *Publishers*
London and Philadelphia

First published in 2019
by Jessica Kingsley Publishers
73 Collier Street
London N1 9BE, UK
and
400 Market Street, Suite 400
Philadelphia, PA 19106, USA

www.jkp.com

Library of Congress Cataloging in Publication Data
Names: Cowie, Helen, author. | Tenenbaum, Harriet, author. | Jones, Ffion,
author.
Title: Emily is being bullied, what can she do? : a story and anti-bullying
guide for children and adults to read together / Helen Cowie, Harriet
Tenenbaum and Ffion Jones.
Description: London ; Philadelphia : Jessica Kingsley Publishers, 2018.
Identifiers: LCCN 2018023842 | ISBN 9781785925481
Subjects: LCSH: Bullying in schools--Prevention--Juvenile literature. |
Bullying--Prevention--Juvenile literature
Classification: LCC LB3013.3 .C689 2018 | DDC 371.5/8--dc23
LC record available at https://lccn.loc.gov/2018023842

British Library Cataloguing in Publication Data
A CIP catalogue record for this book is available from the British Library

ISBN 978 1 78592 548 1
eISBN 978 1 78450 948 4

Printed and bound in Great Britain

MIX
Paper from
responsible sources
FSC® C013056

To Finley, Isabella, Rosa, Arabella and Samuel

Contents

How to use this book

This book can be used by parents or teachers as a helpful resource to discuss bullying. The first part of the book is a fictional story about a child who is bullied at school, with a focus on different ways of ending the bullying. The second part of the book is a guide for adults and includes definitions of bullying that put the behaviour in its larger context, suggestions for ways to help children prevent and resolve bullying situations, and further resources for parents and teachers.

The book highlights that bullying is never the fault of the child being bullied. However, children who are being bullied might find some of the story and pictures upsetting. We recommend that you read the book first before you read it together with your child or students. When you read it together, take time to discuss the ideas and feelings evoked. You may wish to ask questions about how the main character feels and how the school and other children might help to resolve the situation. This may help to reinforce the book's positive message that everyone can make a difference in the bullying situation.

Emily

Hello. My name is Emily and I have been bullied.

I'd like to tell you how I was bullied, what it felt like and what helped make it stop.

What is bullying?

I didn't know what the word "bullying" really meant until it started happening to me. I thought it was being beaten up or being threatened. Sometimes it is, but really bullying is when someone hurts or upsets someone else on purpose, again and again over time.

Some children pick on people to make themselves feel better, because bullying is about power. Sometimes they are actually bigger or stronger, but sometimes they just know how to make themselves popular. They pick on people using this power so that they can feel more powerful, usually because they don't feel that they have power in other parts of their lives.

What happened when I was bullied

I didn't even know I was being bullied at first. It just happened one break time that no one would play with me. Eventually, someone told me that a girl called Hannah had been spreading rumours about me. I've known

Hannah a long time, but we've never been friends. I didn't know why she would say mean things about me and so I thought it must be a mistake. I didn't think it was going to be a problem.

But Hannah was popular, so people seemed to listen to her. Soon, I didn't have anyone to play with.

Hannah and her friends would whisper when I went past and sometimes they would hiss words at me, like "weird" and "ugly". Hannah started calling me "Smellily" when the teacher wasn't around. I thought it was a stupid name, but it still upset me.

In the hallway, Hannah and her friends would push past me, knocking my bag out of my hands. They would smile and say "Sorry!" in a sarcastic voice, but I knew they were doing it on purpose.

Some people laughed when it happened, but most of them just watched and said nothing. Nobody helped me pick up my bag and no one stuck up for me. I didn't understand why everyone seemed to be taking Hannah's side over mine.

I wished I was invisible.

How I felt when I was bullied

At school

I started to hate going to school. It felt like everyone was looking at me all the time and talking about me behind my back.

I'd try to keep my head down and keep myself to myself.

I didn't even want to be with people like Beth and Ravi, who I've known forever. I thought we were friends, but they weren't standing up for me, so now I wasn't so sure. I wondered if they had ever really liked me, or maybe I had done something that had put them off me. I couldn't think what it could be. Maybe I *was* weird, like everyone said.

Because I didn't know why the bullying was happening, I didn't know what to do about it. It was so confusing.

I was scared.

I didn't have anyone to talk to about it and so it felt like the problem was getting bigger and bigger.

I kept going to the school nurse. I said it was because I felt sick and I had a headache. I did – a bit – but mainly it was because it meant I could miss class. I couldn't concentrate in class anyway because I kept worrying about what was going to happen at lunch time.

But then the teachers started to notice I wasn't doing too well and that got me worried. School felt like the only thing I was really good at and now I wasn't even good at that. I started to hate even being there and I didn't even stay for my after-school clubs, like hockey and Spanish. I used to really enjoy them, but I just wanted to get away as soon as possible.

At home

I suppose it should have been a relief to be at home and away from the situation with Hannah, but it wasn't like that. I couldn't stop thinking about what was happening at school.

At night, I couldn't get to sleep because I'd go over and over the situation at school, thinking about what this person said or that person did. When I finally fell asleep, I'd have nightmares about everything that was happening with Hannah. Staying up late and not sleeping properly meant I was tired and cross all day. All I wanted to do was stay in my room. I didn't even want to get out of bed in the mornings. I started saying I was sick so that I wouldn't have to go to school or join in with family time. Even at the weekend all I wanted to do was stay in my room, because I was already worrying about Monday.

Just thinking about school made me feel sick. Mum kept asking if I was OK and even though I knew she was worried, I was embarrassed about the whole situation and would tell her to leave me alone. I thought that I was the problem, so I was the one who had to fix it. I thought that I had to handle it all myself.

My little brother tried to cheer me up by playing with me, but I'd just shout at him. I felt so angry and upset all the time. It felt like I would always feel like this.

What I thought about when I was being bullied

One of the main things I'd think about when I was being bullied was "Why me?" I couldn't think of anything I'd done that might make people think I was a bad person who deserved to be treated this way.

Because I couldn't think of anything I'd done to deserve being bullied, I thought it was because of who I was. I'm not perfect, but I think I'm nice to people. I'm a bit quiet and shy but people say they like that about me. I wondered if maybe it was because I liked putting my hand up when the teacher asked questions. So I stopped doing that, but the bullying carried on anyway.

Mum and Dad always call me "special". Being special suddenly felt really bad, as if it was just another word for weird.

I kept on wishing I was someone else.

What I did to help myself

When the bullying carried on after I'd tried so hard to fit in, I started to get more and more angry.

Why were they still picking on me?

One day, I got really angry and pushed Hannah back when she pushed past me in the hallway. I didn't care if she got angry with me, I just wanted to lash out.

But then she did something worse than push back. She laughed at me, and then her friends did too.

I felt so stupid and helpless. Somehow, I'd made things worse. It gave them an excuse to be even more mean.

I had to come up with another way of dealing with it. I remembered what I'd heard my dad tell my brother when he'd been laughed at in the playground.

"Just ignore it and act like you don't care", he'd said. So, that's what I tried to do. I would walk past them and act as if I hadn't heard the mean things they were saying.

It seemed to work for a while. They didn't seem to be laughing at me as much.

But I still didn't have any friends. It's difficult to pretend you're too busy to take any notice when it's just you walking around the playground.

And the truth was that I still felt very upset.

In some ways, the whispering was worse than the laughing and the names. They never seemed to get told off when it was "just" whispering.

I'd also heard that instead of crying or hitting back, being assertive can help.

I knew that being assertive wasn't the same as being aggressive – I'd already found out that made things worse. Being assertive, I think, meant staying calm and standing up for myself.

So, one lunch break, I gave it a try.

One girl whispered, "Your hair looks rubbish as usual." I should have been used to it by now, but I felt like crying straight away.

I didn't, though. Instead, I looked the girl straight in the eye and said, in a calm, clear voice, "That's your opinion, but I like my hair like this." I walked away before she could say anything else. I felt better!

I kept on practising looking confident and acting assertively and it did start to help.

Even if I felt nervous inside, I wouldn't let anyone see it. I'd keep my back straight and my head high, instead of being hunched over and looking at the floor. I practised speaking with a strong, calm voice and I think I sounded more confident.

It did actually seem to make a difference.

I was starting to think that maybe I'd found the solution and maybe I'd got the best of the bullies, but then it all got worse. Hannah's group and some other kids from other classes started to push me around at lunch time. I guess I wasn't reacting to their nasty words in the way they wanted me to, so they thought they'd try pushing me and pulling my hair instead.

They said it was a "game" and a "joke" but it wasn't funny. It actually hurt.

I decided this time to walk away, but they knew that they had got to me. Sometimes, you just can't pretend everything is OK, even if you want to.

I realized that I couldn't handle this situation by myself any more. I was all out of ideas and I needed help. I was scared to say anything in case it made things worse. But deep down, I knew that things would only change for good if I told someone what was happening.

People who helped

At home

When Mum picked me up after school that day, I burst into tears. I didn't want to tell her what was going on, but I was so unhappy I couldn't keep it to myself any more. I didn't want her or Dad to worry and I thought I should be able to sort it out myself, but it all just came flooding out.

She hugged me for a long, long time. She said she had known that something was going on but couldn't do anything until I told her what it was.

It was such a relief to tell her. She said that I didn't have to cope with it alone any more. It wasn't my fault. And we'd work it out together.

She said she was going to ring the school to get the situation sorted out, but I asked her not to. I wasn't sure yet if that's what I wanted. I just felt better now that I knew she was on my side.

At school

At school, I started to realize that people were on my side too. The nurse called me in to her office because I kept going to her with tummy aches and headaches. She asked me what was wrong.

She was so nice, I felt OK about telling her what was happening.

She said the same as Mum – that it wasn't my fault and that it needed to be stopped. It sounds stupid, but I had sort of got used to the bullying and thought it was just something I had to put up with. The idea that it might actually stop felt weird and unreal. The nurse asked me if I wanted to tell my teacher what had been happening. She told me that they would both help to sort this out.

It was scary, but my teacher was so nice when I told her. She said we could have some special sessions in class, if I didn't mind, to talk about bullying. At first, I wasn't sure about that. I didn't want people to think that I was a tell-tale, but the teacher promised that it would help. I didn't think anything could make it worse, so I said yes.

I was so nervous when the whole class got together. The teacher asked the rest of the class how someone who is being bullied might feel. Everyone must have known what was happening to me and I was expecting them to say mean things, but they didn't. Lucy said that it must make that person feel very lonely and Marcus said bullying wasn't nice or fair.

Hearing that made me feel a bit better and when it was my turn to talk, I felt more confident.

When I started to speak, I felt like the words were catching in my throat. But I knew I had to tell the truth.

"I think that someone being bullied feels lonely and thinks that no one cares about them, especially if everyone joins in or doesn't say anything to help. I think they feel very confused and sad too, because they think there must be a reason they're being picked on. But there's never a good reason to pick on someone else, so they won't ever get an answer."

The teacher said that was a good answer
and then moved on to the next person. I had
been staring at the carpet when I said it, but I
snuck a glance at Hannah. She looked different
now. I couldn't tell if she was sad, or angry,
or working out how to get me after class. But
I didn't think it mattered, because whatever
happened, I knew I wasn't alone and if

something did happen, that there were things I could do about it and people who would help me.

As the special sessions continued every week, I felt more and more supported in the group. I feel so much happier and more confident now. One of the main things that changed was when people, including my own friends, started to be nice to me. They've helped me to realize that I'm not on my own and that it wasn't my fault that I was bullied.

I know it's OK to ask for help and every day I still practise acting in a more assertive way.

If it happens again in the future, I know exactly what to do.

Hannah:
The perspective of the child doing the bullying

I know I'm not always very nice to people, and I guess I feel a bit ashamed about what I've been doing to the other kids. But it's all meant to be just for fun.

Being at school is about the only time I get to have fun. I hate being at home. Mum and Dad are never there and, when they are, they just shout all the time.

My big brother, Jack, is just the same. He shouts all the time too. He's always calling me "fat" and "ugly" and he always breaks my things.

Mum and Dad just laugh when he does it and even though they tell Jack to stop, it doesn't seem like they mean it. Nothing ever happens to him because of the mean things he does, so he just carries on.

The other day we had something called Circle Time at school. The teacher asked us, "How do you think someone who is being

bullied might feel?" Everyone took turns
to speak.

This girl, Emily, who I guess I've picked
on a bit, said it made her feel really sad and
confused. When I heard her saying that, I
felt kind of weird. She's sort of quiet and
kind of a swot, so she was an easy person to
tease. I guess teasing her made me feel more
confident for a bit. Especially when my friends
laughed. But, I suppose, me and my friends
didn't know how bad Emily was feeling.
Or maybe we did, but it was easier to ignore
it. It's all pretty confusing and I don't know
how to feel about myself now. I don't
think I'm bad, but I realize I've been doing
bad things.

I hadn't really thought much about
that before.

When it was my turn to speak in Circle Time, I said, "pass", because I was too embarrassed to say anything. Everyone must have seen my cheeks starting to go red. I know Emily did, because she looked over at me.

I realized I had to say sorry to Emily, but I didn't know how to do it. After class, I went to talk to one of the other teachers, who I know from outside school. I was worried that she would tell me off, but she listened to me and asked if I wanted to change the way I treated people. I realized that I did, so she's helping me to work out why I acted like that.

Picking on people doesn't really make me feel any better deep down. I actually feel upset that I've made other people feel so bad.

The teacher says realizing that is a big first step. She's making me see that I can change and that I don't need to hurt other people any more.

Beth and Ravi: The perspectives of the bystanders

Me and Ravi both felt bad that our friend Emily was having a hard time. We hadn't joined in with the bullying, but we had both kept quiet and hadn't stuck up for Emily.

There was one time before a gym lesson when Hannah hid Emily's gym kit.

We all saw where she'd hidden it, but nobody told Emily. Me and Ravi felt really uncomfortable when Emily got told off, but Hannah is so popular and everyone was laughing so we didn't say anything. We didn't want her to do it to us next.

It always felt easier to stay quiet and walk the other way. But after hearing Emily in Circle Time saying how lonely she was, I suddenly felt really bad. I could see Ravi did too.

When Emily spoke at Circle Time, she said that the worst bit was everyone joining in or people like us not saying anything at all. She said it made her feel really lonely – like no one cared.

Me and Ravi looked at each other and felt really guilty. We do care about her, but we hadn't said anything because we were scared that we'd get picked on, too. We didn't want to stand out.

We both realized that even if we hadn't laughed or said mean things, we'd been taking part in the bullying by not saying anything.

At break after Circle Time, when we saw Emily sitting on her own on the buddy bench, we decided to be brave, even though we were scared of what Hannah might say. We went over and sat down next to her. She looked so relieved.

We both felt relieved too. We realized just
how bad we had been feeling by not standing
up for her. When we were sitting next to
Emily, we felt proud and so much happier.

Information for adults

This chapter is intended mainly as a guide for adults (e.g. parents, teachers, other professionals).

What is bullying?

Bullying happens when:

- a child hurts or upsets another child on purpose

- the behaviour is done more than once and over time

- one child has more power than the other child (e.g. is stronger or more popular).

It is not bullying when one child has a single argument or fight with another child who is of equal strength or power. In the story, Emily is continually bullied on multiple occasions by different people and in a variety of ways.

What are the different types of bullying?

Emotional bullying: e.g. name-calling, spreading rumours, making fun of someone, commenting on a child's appearance in an unkind way.

Indirect bullying: e.g. leaving a child out of games, not inviting them to parties, not sitting with them at lunch times, asking other children not to play with that child.

Physical attacks on another child: e.g. hitting, kicking, pushing, pulling hair.

Physical attacks on a child's property: e.g. stealing lunch money, damaging books, throwing school bags around, drawing on another child's clothing, hiding gym kit.

Cyberbullying: emotional or indirect bullying using an electronic device, such as a mobile phone or tablet. This type of bullying tends to affect older children who usually have more access to electronic devices.

What roles do children play in bullying?

When bullying happens, children play different "roles" – a role is the way a person behaves in a situation. These behaviours can be changed and, sometimes, children play more than one of the roles (e.g. sometimes a child may be bullied and bully others, like Hannah in the story who is bullied at home).

Bully: the child who hurts another child, either emotionally or physically.

Victim: the child who is being bullied.

Bully-victim: the child who is bullied and bullies others.

Defender: the child who steps in to help and protect the victim.

Assistants to the bully: the children who help the bully to harm other children.

Reinforcers of the bully: the children who cheer on and encourage the bully.

Outsiders/bystanders: the children who watch the bullying situation and do not step in to help the child being bullied.

Who is at risk of being bullied?

Any child is potentially at risk of being bullied. However, children who are particularly vulnerable to being bullied are perceived as being different from their peers in some way. This could include children with special needs or disabilities, children of a different race, children who are perceived as being weak, sensitive, or having low self-esteem, children who are less popular than others, or children with any other perceived "difference". In the story, Emily isn't particularly different from her peers but she is perceived as being weaker and an easy target because she acts in a passive rather than assertive way. Whilst acting passively can often mean the bullying continues, what is important to remember is that the child being bullied is never to blame.

What are the signs to look out for?

Children may not want to tell anyone if they are being bullied because they are scared it will get worse, or they are embarrassed, or they think it may be their fault. Sometimes, there are no outward indications that a child is being bullied but if you suspect bullying, there are some signs to look out for. These include:

- losing confidence or being easily upset, nervous or withdrawn
- other changes in behaviour such as being moody, aggressive, or angry at home
- worrying about going to school
- not doing as well at school
- frequently complaining of stomach aches or headaches
- not sleeping well
- coming home with damaged or lost belongings
- physical injuries.

If a child is exhibiting one of more of these signs, it does not necessarily mean that they are being bullied but these are useful signs to look out for if you suspect something is wrong.

What are the effects of being bullied?

- As we have seen in Emily's story, being the target of bullying can have a very negative impact on children's emotional wellbeing. They may feel that no one cares about them and no one is interested in their suffering.

- Being the target of bullying can also have a negative impact on the child's capacity to learn. As demonstrated by Emily's story, school work can very often suffer.

- Children who are being bullied are much more likely to become socially isolated, as they may withdraw from relationships in the peer group. Over time, this means they become less able to engage with the social life of the school and with the learning processes in the classroom. This can lead to feelings of low self-esteem, depression and anxiety.

- As a result of these feelings, they may resort to ineffective coping strategies, such as denial, refusal to think about the incidents of bullying, or staying away from school. In the most extreme cases, some children may resort to self-harm as a way of dealing with emotional pain. There are organizations that can offer advice, including Childline in the UK (www.childline.org.uk) and StopBullying in the US (www.stopbullying.gov).

As the effects of being bullied can last through childhood and adolescence into adulthood, it is crucial for schools, parents and other adults to recognize the needs of children who are being bullied and to provide opportunities for them to be heard and understood.

What to tell children if they are being bullied?

- Explain what bullying is, with a focus on behaviour rather than labelling the children involved and blaming others. Sometimes, like Hannah in the story, a child who bullies has a difficult home life and doesn't think highly of themselves. Often children who bully are insecure and bully to feel more powerful. By avoiding labelling a child a "bully" or "victim" and instead referring to them as "the child who bullied" and "the child who was bullied", this sends the message that the child's behaviour can be changed.

- Make sure that children know that for bullying to occur it must be on purpose, occur more than once, and that there is often a power imbalance.

- Explain that it is not their fault that they have been bullied. No one ever deserves to be bullied.

- Rather than saying, "sort it out yourself" or "ignore it", which can be very hard to do when you are being bullied and gives the message that bullying has to be tolerated, make sure they know that you want to talk about their day and that you are open to discussing their feelings, both positive and negative. Encouraging open discussion will make them feel like their voice is being heard, that you are interested in what is going on, and that they are not alone. It will often seem scary for them to speak out, but by being supportive and listening calmly, you will give them the message that they can trust you.

What other ways can you help at home?

- As we have seen in the story, Emily is a target because she acts passively rather than assertively. Assertive behaviour can be learnt and practised over time. Adults can model assertiveness by expressing their feelings in a calm, respectful and non-aggressive way. Role playing with children is a good way of helping them to practise portraying confidence through their words and body language. Once children are taught the skills of assertive communication, they are better equipped to deal with situations such as bullying.

- Children are also better able to cope with bullying if they have another outlet. For example, they could be encouraged to join an out-of-school club where they can make different friends and focus on an activity that they enjoy or are good at. This helps to prevent bullying from being the only focus in their lives and also improves their confidence. Encourage any activity that develops self-esteem as this will help to counteract the feelings of worthlessness caused by being the target of bullying.

- If your child opens up, listen to what they are telling you without getting angry. Let them know you are on their side and ask them how they would like you to help before rushing in and acting on what they have told you. As in Emily's story, children may not be ready for you to approach the school immediately. You can explain that it may be better to talk to the school but that you won't take action until you have discussed it with them. If they are happy for you to discuss the situation with the teacher or head teacher, be firm but polite, focusing on behaviour rather than blaming the other child.

- If the bullying continues, keeping a bullying incident diary can be helpful to record the bullying accurately with dates and events. When the school is shown the diary, also record what actions the school takes and ask for follow-up meetings to see if things are improving.

- Never tell a child to fight back because, as we have seen in Emily's story, this can make things worse and can also lead to the school seeing the targeted child as the problem. Instead, work with the school to try to make the bullying stop. Encourage the child to identify and talk to a trusted adult in school such as a teacher or school nurse if the bullying happens again. Often, the school nurse is considered by students to be outside the academic system and so able to provide non-judgemental support and advice. They are also trained to be alert to physical symptoms that may be indicated by children who are being bullied such as stomach aches and headaches. The school nurse has an important role in the prevention of bullying.

How can schools help to stop bullying?

In many countries, schools are legally required to have an anti-bullying policy – that is, a set of measures in place to prevent bullying. Check if your school has an anti-bullying policy. Things to note would include the following key points.

Schools should:

1. **listen** to students, carers and parents

2. **include** us all, including those with special educational needs and disabilities

3. **respect** everyone in the school

4. **challenge** all forms of discriminatory language, including disablist, misogynous, racist and homophobic language

5. **celebrate difference**

6. **understand** what bullying is and isn't

7. **believe** all students and take them seriously when they report incidents of bullying

8. **have a widely publicized system for reporting, monitoring and recording** bullying that all children, parents, carers and staff know how to use

9. **take action** in response to all incidents of bullying

10. **have clear policies** that are widely and actively promoted in the school, to parents and carers, and to all staff.

An effective school anti-bullying policy will be actively reviewed and adapted over time in partnership with children, teachers, healthcare professionals and parents. Schools where anti-bullying policies are working well often have a positive school climate. School climate is the general feeling of a school – the degree to which it is friendly and welcoming or impersonal and unfriendly. In schools with a positive climate, there is an emphasis on cooperation and supportive relationships among the children. Schools with a negative school climate are more likely to have higher rates of bullying.

As well as anti-bullying policies, many schools also offer different types of support to help stop bullying – some targeted at the victims, some at the children doing the bullying, and some at the entire school. We have seen examples of some of the support offered by schools in Emily's story. Here are some widely used methods of support:

- **Circle Time:** As in Emily's story, children sit in a circle where they are given the opportunity to express their feelings and thoughts about issues of concern to them. The circle is a safe place in which to practise new skills and to work out new ways of responding to difficult situations. A prop can be used: the "magic microphone", which is passed around the circle. The student who is speaking holds the magic microphone, which helps the other students to concentrate on what they are saying.

- **Peer support:** Peer supporters are trained to offer active listening and support to the child being bullied. Older peer supporters can run workshops to a whole class on such issues as forming new friendships, taking action against bullying, resolving everyday conflicts or making the transition to a new school.

• **Befriending:** This is an informal type of peer support. Here children volunteer to offer friendship and support to other children who are at risk of being bullied. Befrienders look out for children who may be isolated or alone. Some schools have a friendship bench for children who may be feeling sad or lonely; befrienders will look out for children on the bench to offer them friendship and support.

• **Support groups:** Here children form a group that includes children who have been doing the bullying; bystanders and children who have been bullied. They explore a bullying situation and discuss ways of resolving it, without blaming anyone.

• **Restorative practice:** Here the child who has been bullying others is given the opportunity to acknowledge the harm that they have done to another child, to take responsibility for the damage that they have done, to accept that action needs to be taken to change the situation, and to agree to certain actions that will prevent such bullying taking place in the future.

• **Whole school policy (WSP) against bullying:** Typically this involves clear rules that have been negotiated with adults and children in the school community. These rules are likely to be perceived as fair by the children. The school will also have a clear system for reporting, recording and monitoring incidents of bullying and making good communication with the relevant parents.

- **Active celebration of diversity** in all aspects of the curriculum, e.g. in history, languages, personal, social and health education, and school assemblies. Teachers can use any aspect of the curriculum to discuss issues relating to diversity.

- **Counselling:** In serious cases of bullying the school can arrange for trained counsellors to provide confidential support on a one-to-one basis using a non-judgemental approach. This enables the child who has been bullied to develop ways to respond to the bully and to explore strategies for becoming emotionally stronger.

- **Sanctions:** These are usually the last resort when everything else has failed to make changes. Disciplinary methods are usually only applied to children who persistently bully their peers. They must be applied fairly, taking into account the characteristics of the child who bullies. The disciplinary action gives a clear message that the child's *behaviour* is unacceptable and that it must not happen again. When all sanctions have failed to change the behaviour, it may be necessary to exclude that child permanently from the school. This does not tend to happen except in the most serious cases of bullying.

How can you encourage other children to help?

As we have seen in Emily's story, children who watch the bullying situation and say nothing are reinforcing the message that bullying is OK. Most children, like Beth and Ravi in the story, feel uncomfortable watching bullying but don't know how to help. They also often don't realize that they are taking part in the bullying by not saying anything. The more children that stand by and say nothing, the less likely it is that anyone will help the child being bullied. This is called the "bystander effect". It is, therefore, important for so-called "bystanders" to realize that they can make a huge difference to the child being bullied. This is particularly the case when more than one child gets involved; a group of children standing up to the child doing the bullying gives a powerful message that bullying won't be tolerated. As we have seen, children are often reluctant to say anything because they don't want to get picked on themselves or stand out in any way. However, children can be encouraged by schools and parents to take a more active and positive role. Once they have been taught the skills, they are better equipped to know what to do if a bullying incident arises. Here are some ways to encourage them to get more involved:

- Talk with children about how a child who has been bullied feels to encourage them to offer support.

- Encourage them to persuade other children to get involved and stand up to bullying alongside them. This tends to have more effect on the child doing the bullying and also means it is less likely that the child who is standing up to the bullying will become the next target of bullying.

- Explain the difference between "telling tales" (or "tattling") when a child tries to get another child in trouble for a small incident which is not hurting themselves or others, and "reporting" an incident to help someone because they are being bullied.

- Help them to recognize what bullying looks like so that they know when they should intervene or get help.

- Encourage children to be kind to the child being bullied and to include them in their activities and games. One friend is sometimes all a targeted child needs to start to make them feel better. It may also help to reduce the incidents of bullying as children who bully tend to target those who are on their own a lot and do not have a circle of friends to stand up for them. Even if the bystander feels too afraid to speak up against the child doing the bullying during the incident, explain to them that simply asking the child who is being bullied if they are OK after the incident is also a way of helping. It makes the targeted child feel that they are not on their own.

- Role play with children at home or in class so that they know what to say and how to act if a bullying situation arises. The better prepared they are, the more likely they are to take a stance when an incident does occur.

- Help them to identify trusted adults at school that they can report an incident to or go to for help. Children need to know that they should only step in if it is safe for them to do so and that help is nearby if needed.

As we have seen, bystanders can make a massive difference. Therefore, it is important to empower children by teaching them ways to take action against bullying. It is when everyone starts to work together that the incidence of bullying can be reduced.

Resources

United Kingdom
Anti-Bullying Alliance (ABA)
The Anti-Bullying Alliance was founded by NSPCC and the NCB. ABA develops and shares good practice in schools and the community. They have a wide range of resources on their website.

www.anti-bullyingalliance.org.uk

Bullying UK
Provides useful resources about bullying and cyberbullying.

www.bullying.co.uk

Childline
Provides free confidential advice for children on a range of issues, including bullying.

www.childline.org.uk

National Children's Bureau (NCB)

A UK charity whose aim is to reduce inequalities that prevent children from realizing their full potential. The NCB website has a wide range of resources on the prevention and reduction of bullying, including the Anti-Bullying Alliance (see above).

www.ncb.org.uk

National Society for the Prevention of Cruelty to Children (NSPCC)

The NSPCC website has a wide range of advice and resources for children and young people, and for adults concerned about a child's wellbeing. Also includes the Anti-Bullying Alliance (see above).

www.nspcc.org.uk

The Diana Award Anti-Bullying Campaign

The Diana Award Anti-Bullying Ambassadors programme empowers children to be active in changing the behaviour and attitudes of their peers with regard to bullying. It trains and supports anti-bullying ambassadors. There are good general resources and inspiring videos on their website.

www.antibullyingpro.com

United States

Pacer Kids Against Bullying

Pacer Kids Against Bullying hosts a child-friendly website designed for elementary school children to learn about how to prevent bullying. It also has useful guidance for parents and teachers.

www.pacerkidsagainstbullying.org

stopbullying.gov
A US federal government website providing useful resources, including videos, for the prevention and reduction of bullying in schools.

www.stopbullying.gov

Australia
Bullying. No Way!
An Australian website developed by educators to help schools create learning environments where children are safe from bullying.

www.bullyingnoway.gov.au